Table of Contents

Letter from the Editor ... 1
Katie Haegele

Haunted-House Cat ... 3
Vanessa Berry

Thank You Lucy and Sketch ... 6
Jay McQuirns

Spring, At Home ... 10
Joe Carlough

Clover ... 11
Jackie Soro

Two Nilla Comics ... 16
Missy Kulik

Cat & Pie Go on a Walk ... 18
Defectivepudding

Escape ... 24
Helen Kaucher

Letter from the Editor

Hi there! Since you've picked up this zine I'm guessing you're a cat lover, so please, come on in and join the Cat Party.

This party got started a few years ago, when I wrote a book of stories about all the cats I've ever met. Before it came out the publisher, Microcosm, put out a zine of excerpts from the book. Once these pieces of writing were out there in the world, I noticed I kept getting the same response from people who read them: *They* wanted to tell *me* their cat stories. One after the other, people pulled up photos of their cats on their phones, rolled up their sleeves to show me cat tattoos, and told me in loving detail about the funny thing their cat has taken to doing. I decided it would be fun to invite other people to share their cat tales, so Microcosm and I have continued publishing these zines as a series, most of which have been anthologies of work by different writers and artists.

As you might guess, I have a lot of *feelings* about cats. Feelings and thoughts. One of the things I've always thought about cats is how intertwined they are with the place where they live, and how intimate that is. Even if they're sometimes allowed out of the house, cats are *of* the house. Draped over the back of the couch, sitting like a sphinx on the kitchen floor: They *inhabit*. If you have a friend with a dog, you've probably bumped into them and their dog on a walk through the neighborhood. Dogs get out and about; you see them in parks and in the backseat of the vehicles they get carted around in. But if your friend has cats instead, you'll only spend time with them if you get invited over. It's possible the cat won't even come out of hiding while you're there, but his spirit brightens the space nonetheless, like a little flame.

I've been thinking a lot about the idea of home lately, since god knows I've been here all the time. My home is a row house (known to people in other parts of the world as a townhouse or a terraced house) in a residential neighborhood in Philadelphia. I live here with my little family, which consists of my husband Joe and our dear cat, Coco, a chubby, chocolate-point Siamese with two back feet like a jack rabbit's that she likes to stick out behind her when she's lounging around. In fact she's doing that right now, directly behind my desk chair as I write this, both of us letting the fan blow cool air over our bods on a hot July morning.

Having the entertainment and comfort of this cat's company always means a lot to me, but during this pandemic I'm even more aware of how important she is to my sense of well-being. All day long Joe and I comment on her habits as though they're fascinating. *Look! The cat's sleeping next to her water bowl again!* Watching her saunter in and out of rooms is one of my favorite hobbies. Every time I gaze at the precious brown fuzz on her feet, it's like the first time. Loving my cat never gets old.

That being said, I'm pretty sure Coco is getting tired of us. Early in the quarantine she seemed confused. She'd walk back and forth, looking at us and squawking like she does when she's in a mood (which is most of the time). *Why are you still here?* she seemed to be saying. More recently, she's taken to napping on the house's stuffy top floor, wedged behind a rack of clothing in a corner. We've calculated this corner as the absolute furthest point from the front room where Joe and I hang out that she could find and still be in the same house. It's got me wondering why, exactly, she wants to have the house to herself. Could she be seeing Steven, the sexy striped tabby up the street who swaggers around like he owns the block? Maybe she just misses her alone time, or wishes she could be even more unselfconscious when she slurps water, belches (yes, really), or sleeps with all four legs sticking straight out, like a horse.

Cats or no cats, in an ideal world your home is a sanctuary, a place where you can be safe. I really hope this is true for you. I know it's not like that for everyone. Some of us don't have a regular bed to sleep in, a place to call home, and are even more vulnerable now than before. Others have homes that they have to leave in order to work jobs that might not feel safe. We all have unique situations, some much more challenging than others, and yet the same heavy thing is pressing down on all of us.

I wish I could say that our shared situation has made me feel closer to everyone, but that's only sometimes true. Between the ever-present systems of oppression doing their work on us and the shit-ass presidential administration we're currently dealing with, there are a lot of forces working to divide us.

But I'm not having it! I'm gonna keep reaching out, keep writing these zines, these letters to the universe—to you. I may not have a lot to offer, but I'm giving it with all my heart. Because I miss all of you, even the ones I haven't met. I hope we'll meet again, or meet for the first time, one day soon. Until then, keep loving, keep fighting, and keep hugging your cats.

Katie —July 2020

Katie Haegele is a writer and longtime zine maker from Philadelphia. She has published many essays and book reviews in print and online publications, as well as two books of creative nonfiction and a collection of essays. Together with her husband Joe Carlough, she runs a zine collection and performance space called the East Falls Zine Reading Room. Visit her online at www.thelalatheory.com.

Haunted-House Cat
Vanessa Berry

Most of the neighbourhoods around where I live have a few houses that are conspicuously run-down, in need of paint and repair, and surrounded by overgrown gardens. These houses are fascinating in the same way as old photograph albums are, the kind you might find discarded, or for sale in an antique store. The people in the photographs inside such albums are strangers, but there's something familiar and captivating about them, the way their lives seem to be both like, and unlike, yours.

If you look closely as you pass by these houses, you'll most likely see cats hanging around. Cats are attracted to places where there are cracks and nooks and places to hide. They lie out amid the long grass of the gardens, or they lounge on the sun-warmed concrete of the front steps or the paths. If you stop and try to coax them over, mostly they just stare back at you, unmoved.

One particular house of this kind is on a corner and is square and painted white. It has a fence that's as irregular as a row of crooked teeth. People stare at it as they walk past, wondering who lives there, and sometimes they point out the black cat with a white chest and feet that sits out the front of it. Some people try to entice her over to them, but there's only one person who can get up close to her, the woman who lives in the house: me.

Every morning when I open the door I look for her. Sometimes she's already there, sitting by the shoes and potted plants on the landing. Or if not she soon appears from a gap in the foundations of the house, trailing cobwebs, blinking her way out of sleep. Good morning Soxy, I say, as she comes up close and pushes her head against my hand, then turns around and nudges me again, and again. Most days start like this, and the scene always feels like the beginning of a fairytale.

Soxy's domain is the earthy, spiderwebbed cavern under my house. Having the wariness of a cat that has never lived with people, she won't come inside, but whenever I go out she appears, as if she has the ability to materialise from thin air. We live our days alongside each other, but I can't claim her as mine in the way of a pet. Instead, I think of her as a companion spirit. During the day as I sit at my desk, she sleeps under the house, curled up in the corner underneath my room, or I can see her through the window, curled up against the fence.

She's a wise cat, a watcher, seeming to register everything that moves through or past the garden which is her domain. She shares it with another cat, her sister Seeka, who is her inverse, white with black patches. Seeka is a less enigmatic character, and round as a marshmallow from the ample feedings by the street's multiple cat ladies. She has little interest in me unless I'm holding a bag of Whiskas, or the "party mix" treats I sometimes give to them. Soxy also has a taste for the party mix, but a lot of the time she is less interested in food than in observing me, as if I'm a puzzle she's continually trying to figure out.

Soxy and Seeka appeared as kittens during the year of the black and white street cats, when their numbers grew into the dozens. Then, to walk down the street at night was to run the gauntlet of their flashing eyes and they would scatter as I approached, so it was as if the shadows were alive. Each had a feature to distinguish it from the others. One had a black patch over an eye, like a pirate. Another had a funny little head, disproportionally small. Another had black and white blotches like it was a miniature Friesian cow. At the peak of the street cat population explosion one of the residents of the apartment building around which they were concentrated progressively rounded them up. She took them to the vet to be desexed before returning and releasing them. Now, seven years later, only a few of the cats from this time remain, those like Soxy and Seeka who have found positions of relative protection, and have people looking out for them.

So, when people ask if I have a cat, I pause. I have Soxy, I reply.

Opening the front door, I see her. She's sitting at the foot of the steps, peering up at me as I look out towards the street. Cars are parked tightly all along it during this time in which everyone's staying at home, waiting out the pandemic lockdown. Another bus goes past, again empty of passengers. With few other sanctioned reasons to be outside, more people than usual are out walking. Almost all of them stare intensely at my house as they go by. But Soxy and I are in our own story, independent of all this. She has cobwebs on her ears from her nights spent in spidery dreamland. I am wearing the black quilted jacket that I've taken to now that I having been spending every day at home. It has deep pockets in which I keep tissues and pens and post-it notes to catch ideas. I move to sit on the front step and Soxy comes up by my side, and we linger here, haunting the house together.

KEEP SMILING!

What's the good of Crying over spilt Milk ? <u>I</u> don't!

Vanessa Berry is a writer and artist and author of the books Mirror Sydney, Ninety9 and Strawberry Hills Forever, and the zine series I am a Camera. She lives and works on unceded Gadigal land in Sydney, Australia. Her website is vanessaberryworld.wordpress.com and she is on Instagram @vanessaberryworld. This vintage postcard hangs above Vanessa's desk.

THANK YOU LUCY AND SKETCH
SKETCH
LUCY
BY JAY McQUIRNS
MARCH 2020
DOESN'T IT FEEL LIKE HE'S AROUND A LOT MORE THAN NORMAL?
IT'S HARD TO SAY. HE'S NOT REALLY MR. SOCIAL BUTTERFLY TO BEGIN WITH.
I DUNNO... SOMETHING'S DIFFERENT.
LET'S GO KNOCK OVER OUR WATER.
YAH!
LATER
WHY ISN'T HE CHASING US?
HE'S BEEN LOOKING OUT THE WINDOW FOR HOURS.

IS THERE A SQUIRREL OUT THERE?!?
SOB SOB
NO... I THINK HE'S CRYING.
UGH... AGAIN.
IT'S YOUR TURN.
YEAH, I KNOW.
MEOW.
APRIL 2020
DO YOU THINK HE'S GONNA MOVE TODAY?
WHO KNOWS? AFTER HE FEEDS US HE SORTA JUST CHECKS OUT.
HE HASN'T GONE OR DONE ANYTHING FOR OVER A MONTH.
YOU MEAN EXCEPT CRY?
OH GOD! DON'T JINX US!

SOB SOB
SHIT.
YOUR TURN.
YEAH, YEAH, YEAH...
MAY 2020
WHAT THE HELL IS ON HIS FACE?
MAYBE HE FINALLY SMELLS YOUR BUTT.
HA HA HA HA HA
WHOA! HE'S GOING OUT.
LET'S GO LAY ON HIS COMICS!!
JUNE 2020

Jay McQuirns spends his days watching dust bunnies intertwine with cat fur in the far reaches of his floor boards. You can follow these exciting escapades on his Instagram @jaymcquirns.

Spring, At Home
poem by Joe Carlough
drawing by Mocha Ishibashi

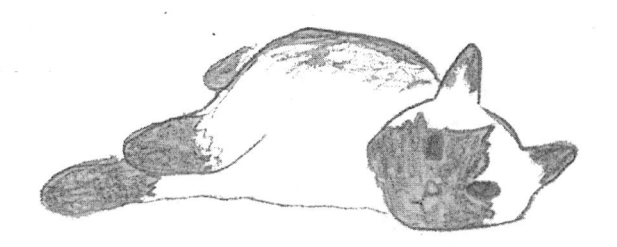

On the first day of spring
we raise all the blinds
we throw open the windows
we open all of the doors
and let the fresh, cool air
course through the house
like the house is breathing

my cat closes her eyes

inhales deeply
exhales deeply

I imitate her and do the same

and for a moment
we are again a part
of the same ecosystem

Joe Carlough runs the zine press Displaced Snail and the cassette label This & That Tapes. He co-runs the East Falls Zine Reading Room with his partner Katie Haegele. He designed and laid out this zine.
displacedsnail.com, thisandthattapes.com, efzrr.com

Mocha Ishibashi currently teaches violin at Little Bow Music and Waseca Montessori, and has performed and recorded with artists like Herbie Hancock, Diana Krall, Christian McBride, Cee Lo, and of Montreal.

A GOOD CAT IS HARD TO FIND

1. AS A LESBIAN, I OPERATE IN A VERY CAT-CENTERED CULTURE.
2. I LOVE CATS.
3. I AM QUITE ALLERGIC TO CATS.

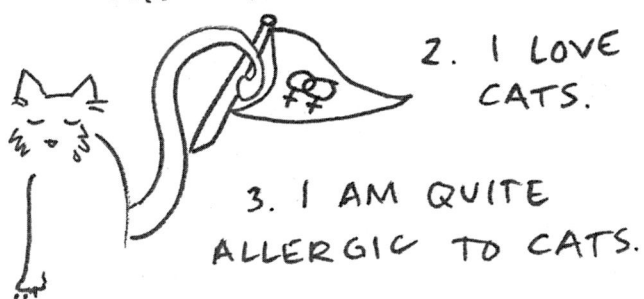

3A. AS SUCH, IT BECOMES NECESSARY FOR ME TO KEEP ANTIHISTAMINES IN MY CAT-LOVING LOVERS' HOMES.

4. CAT LESBIANS ARE PREFERRABLE TO DOG LESBIANS.[1,2]

---

footnotes:

1. IN THE END, DOG LESBIANS WILL CHOOSE THEIR CANINE PARTNER(S) OVER YOU.
2. DOG LESBIANS GET UP TOO EARLY.

5. I HAVE MET THE PERFECT CAT. HER NAME IS GOLDIE AND SHE LIVES IN UPSTATE NEW YORK.

FIG 5A.
GOLDIE LAYING PROVOCATIVELY ON THE FLOOR.

6. I HAVE NOT MET THE PERFECT LOVER.
   - I HAVE LOOKED
   - I'LL KEEP LOOKING
   - MORALE IS LOW

7. I LIED. A GOOD CAT IS NOT HARD TO FIND, THEY'RE EVERYWHERE.

8. THIS FAR INTO QUARATINE I'D RATHER HAVE A CAT, I THINK, THAN A LOVER.

   NB.: EITHER WAY A WARM BODY WOULD BE NICE.

JUNE 2020

ALL CATS ARE BABIES

defund the police

meow

Jackie Soro is an avid zine-maker (and reluctant zine-sharer) who lives, bakes, bikes, plants, plots, and sleeps in West Philadelphia. Jackie, who uses she & they pronouns, is a Sagittarius and a (currently out-of-work) actor/performer. She is currently single and her number is 708-207-5571.

Brushing Nilla

I have to brush the cat. She pretends not to like it, but secretly she does.

purr purr

look at all this fur I brushed off of Nilla.

You should toss that fur outside for birds to use in their nest.

I think I will. That's called "up cycling."

Nilla with Broccoli

each time I make broccoli, Nilla knows.

She sits behind me and waits. Sometimes she paws at me.

Then I hand her the stalk of broccoli. She sniffs it...

sniff sniff

And she likes to chew on it!

Missy Kulik is an illustrator, cartoonist, zine maker, artist, and crafter. Originally from Pittsburgh, currently in Atlanta. Find her online at missykulik.com.

Cat & Pie go on a walk !!!!

BY DEFECTIVEPUDDING

One day a pie was made. But before a piece could cool... it sprouted arms, legs, and a face and ran away!

The pie thought it had escaped death, well at least for that day.

Z Z Z
There also was a witch's apprentice, who was extremely lazy!! Who happened to be asleep when all of a suddon...
a piece of pie ran by!
sniff
sniff
before the pie could pass by
the cat stood up
and said...
Hello my lil pie

where might you be headed this fine day in the Witch's forrest?
GRUMBLE
It's dangerous to travel alone, why don't I help you find a safe spot?
So Cat & Pie walked deeper into the woods to find a safe
SPOT

They walked for a while

The Cat started to sing a tune.

♪ DEEP IN THE WITCH'S WOODS THERE IS A GOOD SPOT FOR FRIENDS TO SPEND! I TOOK MANY FRIENDS THERE. MY FRIEND CREAM, WHO WAS SO PATIENT WITH ME. MY FRIEND MOUSE, WHO I MET IN MY MASTER'S HOUSE. NOW MY NEW FRIEND PIE, WHO I HOPE ISN'T SHY! OFF WE TRAVEL TO MY SECRET SPOT DEEP IN THE WITCH'S WOODS. ♪

Finally in a small clearing with a stump, the cat turned to the pie and said
We are here, my friend!! So sorry for the delay, but you will be safe here; I promise.
GO ahead and take a seat on that stump over there while I fetch some water.

Christa Dippel works under the artist name Defectivepudding. She is a self-taught illustrator and visual artist, and has been pursuing art professionally for several years now. Her works are primarily created in color pencil and graphite. She draws most of her inspiration from vintage media, toys, and clothes, in addition to a fascination with wildlife and nature. As a result, many of her pieces have a nostalgically sweet appearance, even while exploring subjects that are melancholy.

Escape
Helen Kaucher

Ramona has always been a wide-eyed, tumultuous goddess. Since our first meeting at the vet's office, I attributed her looks to a myriad of animals. She was an amalgamation of rabbit, screech owl, weasel, meerkat, panther, dragon, and pygmy marmoset — depending on her mood.

There's no doubt her blood was too wild to be kept indoors.

I bought her a harness and leash to coax her on neighborhood walks, or to spend sunny afternoons basking in the grass. Even being on the porch terrified her, and upon leaving the apartment she would immediately slink towards the door to go back inside. I tried to acclimate her to the harness for a few months, but to no avail. She would remain a windowsill cat.

In mid-March, I began a new stay-at-home discipline. After a week of vacillating between panic, calm, restlessness, and exhaustion, I decided to call the confinement an "Artist in Residence." It felt less foreboding than "quarantine" and held the suggestion that productivity and creativity were lurking within the walls.

My boyfriend Joey and I often joke that our apartment is actually "Ramona's Place." After all, she's there all day every day while we pay her rent and utilities, scoop her poop, and serve her daily meals. It sounds like a pleasant life sentence compared to others, but I imagine such a wild nature stuffed inside her tiny body to be pure anguish.

When I started my new residency, I thought it only fair we share the pronouncement of critical isolation.

Making creative plans started to get exciting, and I was thrilled I had the time to spruce everything up the way I've always wanted. Everything would be kept clean and organized. Each room would look just like every interior decorating catalog I've ever poured over, every cozy living room I'd visited, every studio space I'd seen utilized to its full, angular potential. We would relish in each sunlit room, living in ultimate, green-footed, patchouli-glazed harmony.

The washer and dryer in our building have never been operative since Joey moved in over three years ago. Due to the mechanical inconvenience and our newfound fear of laundromats, I began washing our clothes in the bathtub. Luckily, I am a task-minded human that lives by checklists and learns by action, so this potentially vexing development didn't disturb me. In fact, I began taking pride in my new peasant attitude and humble reliance on fair weather to dry our clothes. I fell in love with the way sunlight bleached our black clothing and how the air permeated the fibers with a sharp feral wind.

One evening I mistakenly grabbed Ramona, who had nestled in a pile of black shirts that I was methodically scooping up to place in the laundry basket. Her little black body was perfectly curled up in our clothing, her glowing eyes widened by my mistake.

When most of my panic-induced busy work around the house became exhausted, I started to germinate seeds on the bedroom windowsills. It's always been a dream of mine to have a fruitful garden plot, but because we rent, I stick to container gardening.

One morning while I was outside transplanting, the owner of the building pulled his utility van into the yard to have a poke around in the basement with the still-useless washer and dryer. After some small talk (which I'd learned now contains more lonely silence, unassuredness, and solidarity than ever before), he motioned to the planters near the stairs and said, "You know, you can have a bigger garden if you'd like."

Permission granted! The next day I dug out a 6'×4' plot near the staircase. Relocating the dirt was a minor issue, but I wound up dumping 120 gallons in the alley next to my neighbor's house. The newly packed dirt mound was a decidedly better neighborhood feature than the plastic gin bottles and broken cinderblocks.

The garden was coming along splendidly. The only fracas present was the neighborhood gang of squirrels that swept through the yard to dig and bury peanuts in any area of loosened soil. Every planter and plot had to be covered with plastic or wire netting to keep them protected and contained.

Ramona and I spent most of the day together. I, at my desk. She, in the window next to me. If I was on the porch, she was on her hind legs peering at me through the screen door. When I tussled around in the garden, I could see her up in the kitchen window — a pair of floating eyes tilting back and forth like the bubble of air inside a spirit level. When we read on the couch in the evenings, Ramona was perched on the pillow near my head, making gentle cooing and sighing sounds while resting her paw on my shoulder.

I rediscovered a love of 10,000 Maniacs, Natalie Merchant, and Tracy Chapman while opting for cheery music to fill the day. Many of the tracks reminded me of my childhood, as my mother had played those albums often. I felt the translucent white curtains of my old living room bellowing through my body; I felt aired out and breezed through, just like the shirts on our clothesline.

One evening, I was making eggplant moussaka and ran out to the porch herb garden to grab some basil leaves. As I opened the door to come inside, Ramona bolted out of the apartment in a fever dash — low and fast. I ran down the steps after her, twisting my ankle and fumbling down the rickety wooden stairs that had swollen in the afternoon heat. I pictured her squished in the road and my heart quickened. There was nowhere sweet enough for her to safely hide in our neighborhood. When I rounded the corner after her, I saw her crouched in a patch of grass, listening to motors whizz by on the main road. Joey ran outside to help corral her, and we managed to trap her in the alley where I had dumped the dirt from the garden. She seemed to have fled regretfully, an assumption I made when Joey told me he saw her peeing while sprinting for refuge. Ramona scurried towards Joey and he was able to grab her while she seized the bone of his forearm in her jaw. As he ran up the steps with her squished against his body, blood trickled onto the planks of our wooden staircase. We washed Joey's arm and prepared for a trip to the hospital to have the bite examined. Before we left, I found Ramona under the dresser and cleaned the blood of her combatant from her forehead.

Masks adorned, we left the hospital and headed to the pharmacy with Joey's arm bandaged up dramatically with layers of gauze to cushion the four pin-sized puncture wounds underneath. "Wonder" by Natalie Merchant was playing throughout the pharmacy when we entered.

Over the next few days, I read up on ways to prevent future cat escapes, which the cat community calls "door dashing." Some tactics a cat owner may implement: The squirt bottle method, greeting and rewarding while distancing from problem zones, entertainment and distraction, hormone therapy, and physical barriers. I settled on entertainment and physical barriers.

Since I already had a surplus of garden netting to keep out the squirrels, I created a homespun child gate and affixed it to the door and wall using velcro. The new installation sectioned off a forbidden triangle of space, making "Ramona's Place" slightly smaller.

Near the end of May, Ramona started to sit near the new gate to smell the fresh air blowing in through the screen, testing her new boundaries. The plants started pushing through their barriers and I fumbled around with netting so the buds wouldn't become strangulated, wondering how much confidence to put in weaves of plastic.

Ramona exemplified that however free our imaginations may be, there is always the desire to flee our physical space, to run in the open air and feel unrestrained or otherwise out of control. I love her more knowing that she still has a wild, undomesticated core. There's a newfound bond we share as we sit together — whether one of us is outside looking in, or inside looking out.

Helen Kaucher (Hels) is an artist in Lancaster County. When she isn't working on products for her business, Hels' Bells Handmade, or experimenting with recycled art and natural materials, she's probably outside or up in a tree somewhere. Find her on Instagram @ohelsbells or on her website: www.helsbellshandmade.com.